S0-BOT-639

HOW TO USE THIS BOOK

Praying together is very important.
This book includes some simple prayers for
children to read and learn at home.

Linda Coates, Cert Ed, MA

My Book of Prayers

illustrated by Louise Barrell

Filmset in Nelson Teaching Alphabet
by kind permission of
Thomas Nelson and Sons Ltd

© MCMLXXXVI by World International Publishing Limited.
All rights reserved throughout the world.
Published in Great Britain by World International Publishing Limited,
An Egmont Company, Egmont House, P.O. Box 111,
Great Ducie Street, Manchester M60 3BL.
Printed in Italy.   SBN 7235 8786 8

Jesus, friend of little children,
At the start of this new day,
Be Thou my guide and helper,
In my work and in my play.

Help me, Lord, to love Thee more
Than I ever loved before,
In my work and in my play,
Be Thou with me through the day.

Thank you for the world so sweet,
Thank you for the food we eat,
Thank you for the birds that sing,
Thank you, God, for everything.

God bless all those that I love;
God bless all those who love me;
God bless the people of every nation,
At home and beyond the sea.

God made the sun
And God made the trees,
God made mountains
And God made me.

O fill my heart with quietness,
When I am deep in prayer,
That I may hear you speak to me
And know that you are there.

We thank Thee, heavenly Father,
Who gives us everything,
Who sends the sunshine and showers,
And makes rich harvest spring.
You clothe the lilies of the field,
And feed each bird and beast;
And all may share Thy tender care,
The greatest and the least.

Loving Jesus, gentle Lamb,
In Thy gracious hands I am.
Make me, Saviour, like Thou art.
Live Thyself within my heart.

Our Father, who art in heaven,
Hallowed be Thy name.
Thy kingdom come,
Thy will be done on earth
as it is in heaven.
Give us this day our daily bread,
And forgive us our trespasses,
As we forgive those that trespass
against us.
And lead us not into temptation,
but deliver us from evil;
For Thine is the kingdom,
the power and the glory,
for ever and ever.
Amen.

All good gifts around us
Are sent from heaven above;
O thank the Lord, O thank the Lord,
For all His love.

I see the moon,
And the moon sees me.
God bless the moon,
And God bless me.

Matthew, Mark, Luke and John,
Bless the bed that I lie on.
Four corners to my bed,
Four angels round my head.
One to sing and one to pray,
And two to watch till break of day.

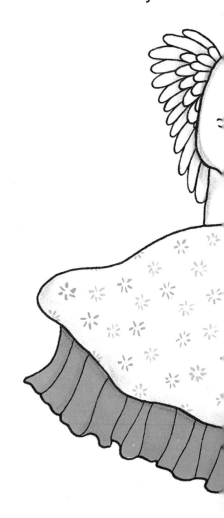